Twin Fla

Guided Journal

60 Days of Gratitude and Self Reflection

This Journal Belongs To

○———————————○

Twin Flame Union Guided Journal

60 Days of Gratitude and Self Reflection

By Gone Goddess

Gone Goddess Publishing
Gone Goddess LLC
gonegoddess.com

"And when we kissed one another for the first time I could swear I heard our souls whisper ever so quietly, 'Welcome home.'"

-Beau Taplin

* Welcome & Instructions *

Blessings and Welcome to the Twin Flame Guided Journal! In these pages you will be implementing a practice of gratitude into your daily life. Gratitude is one of the highest vibrations you can embody, and it instantly aligns you with the abundance of the universe. You will also be diving deep into yourself, uncovering hidden blocks and desires that are preventing your harmonious Re-Union with your twin flame.

*There are 60 daily Journal Exercises, as well as a call to count your blessings. The second half of the gratitude section is a manifestation tool. By thanking the universe for your twin flame union as if you already have it, you will super charge your path to union.

Ex. "I am so grateful that my twin flame and I came together so effortlessly."

[There are blank pages in the back of the book if you need more space.]

*   You will want to set aside at least 15-30 min a day for this practice. If you'd like, you can split up the exercises and do gratitude in the morning, and Journal Prompts in the evening. Find a rhythm and schedule that works for you to maintain a consistent practice. If you skip a day or two, no worries. Simply start again where you left off. If more than a few days go by, you may want to ask yourself:

"What part of me is resistant to committing to this practice?"

Journal for a while answering this question. You may find that a part of you needs some reassurance or comfort in order to continue.

This journal can be used alone, or is an excellent companion to **Same Flames: A Practical Guide to Understanding and Mastering the Twin Flame Path.** If you feel you need more assistance clearing negative patterns or energies that arise during your journaling, reach out to a trusted professional, or visit gonegoddess.com and enroll in Goddess School.

You may encounter some unpleasant or uncomfortable emotions during this journey. Remember that you have to "feel it, to heal it". Stuck or repressed emotions must be first brought to the light of consciousness, and often need to run their full course before they can be released. As always, be gentle with yourself. If at anytime you feel overwhelmed or get stuck in negative emotions, reach out for help.

I love you so much, and I am so grateful that you are here. Commit to this practice and you will experience deep and profound shifts in your reality. Magic you never knew existed will begin making its way into your life. You will gain clarity about the reasons for separation from your beloved, and you will finally find the way back home.

xoxo Gone Goddess

Day One

GRATITUDE

DATE:

TODAY I AM MOST GRATEFUL FOR:

1.

2.

3.

4.

5.

6.

7.

8.

9.

10.

I AM SO GRATEFUL THAT MY TWIN FLAME AND I...

Claiming Union

Write a statement of commitment to your healing journey, to being completely honest and transparent with yourself, and to claiming Your Twin Flame Union now...

Day Two   <u>Gratitude</u   Date:

Today I am Most Grateful for:

1.

2.

3.

4.

5.

6.

7.

8.

9.

10.

I am so grateful that my twin flame and I...

Love List

Write a List of all of the qualities you Desire in your Perfect Mate. You can list physical characteristics, but make sure to spend time focusing on feelings and inherent qualities about their personality and character...

My perfect partner is...

Day Three   <u>Gratitude</u>   Date:

Today I am Most Grateful for:

1.

2.

3.

4.

5.

6.

7.

8.

9.

10.

I am so grateful that my twin flame and I...

Union Script

Imagine that you have been in harmonious Union for some time. Write a short scene or diary entry, and describe in detail how you feel now that you are in harmonious union with your twin flame. Use all of your senses. What do you see? What you do you smell, hear, taste, touch, & feel?

Today my twin and I...

DAY FOUR   GRATITUDE   DATE:

TODAY I AM MOST GRATEFUL FOR:

1.

2.

3.

4.

5.

6.

7.

8.

9.

10.

I AM SO GRATEFUL THAT MY TWIN FLAME AND I...

What's in the Way?

What is blocking your union? You may think you don't know, but answer with the first thing that comes to mind. Speculate or imagine if you must.

I am not in physical union with my twin flame because...

DAY FIVE   GRATITUDE   DATE:

TODAY I AM MOST GRATEFUL FOR:

1.

2.

3.

4.

5.

6.

7.

8.

9.

10.

I AM SO GRATEFUL THAT MY TWIN FLAME AND I...

You are Magnificent

What are your positive attributes? Make a list of all the reasons that you are worthy of love or why someone would benefit from being around you.

I am...

Day Six   <u>Gratitude</u>   Date:

Today I am Most Grateful for:

1.

2.

3.

4.

5.

6.

7.

8.

9.

10.

I am so grateful that my twin flame and I...

Things you Don't love about yourself

Write a list of things you don't love about yourself, or aspects you believe make you unlovable by others.

What are some positive ways that each of those qualities could be applied in life? Where could that same perceived weakness be a strength or an asset?

Day Seven   <u>Gratitude</u   Date:

Today I am Most Grateful for:

1.

2.

3.

4.

5.

6.

7.

8.

9.

10.

I am so grateful that my twin flame and I...

The Original Separation

Close your eyes and take a few deep breaths. Take yourself back to the original lifetime that you separated from your twin flame. Imagine if you have to. Speculate if you must. What do you think happened? Why did you have to leave one another?

The first lifetime we experienced separation...

Day Eight   Gratitude   Date:

Today I am Most Grateful for:

1.

2.

3.

4.

5.

6.

7.

8.

9.

10.

I am so grateful that my twin flame and I...

Past Life Purge

You have probably been feeling emotions surface from remembering your original separation lifetime. Now is the time to purge all of those feelings. Let it all out.

Our original separation made me feel...

Day Nine   <u>Gratitude</u>   Date:

Today I am Most Grateful for:

1.

2.

3.

4.

5.

6.

7.

8.

9.

10.

I am so grateful that my twin flame and I...

New Perspective

Write from the perspective of your twin flame's higher soul. What do they want you to know about that lifetime? Find compassion and forgiveness by listening to their side of the story.

Dear Beloved Twin Flame,

Day Ten   Gratitude   Date:

Today I am Most Grateful for:

1.

2.

3.

4.

5.

6.

.

7.

8.

9.

10.

I am so grateful that my twin flame and I...

Why are you Running?

You may think your twin flame is the runner, but you are both running from something. What are you running to? What are you Running From?

I am running to...

I am running from...

"You and I, we are embers from the same fire, dust from the same star, echoes of the same love."

-Creig Crippen

Twin Flame Tip

Your Twin Flame is Your Perfect Counterpart. They are different but complementary. Who you are and who they are, are a perfect match.

Day Eleven   <u>Gratitude</u>   Date:

Today I am Most Grateful for:

1.

2.

3.

4.

5.

6.

7.

8.

9.

10.

I am so grateful that my twin flame and I...

Core Values

To achieve harmonious union, you need to be clear about what your core values are. Core values are those things that you cannot and will not compromise on. Things like freedom, safety, kindness...etc.

My core values are....

Day Twelve   <u>Gratitude</u>   Date:

Today I am Most Grateful for:

1.

2.

3.

4.

5.

6.

7.

8.

9.

10.

I am so grateful that my twin flame and I...

A picture perfect Life

What does your ideal life look like? Where do you live? Do you have children? What kind of home, car, job, etc?

My ideal life looks like...

Day Thirteen   <u>Gratitude</u>   Date:

Today I am Most Grateful for:

1.

2.

3.

4.

5.

6.

7.

8.

9.

10.

I am so grateful that my twin flame and I...

A perfect feeling life

Twin flame union doesn't always look like howe we thought it would. It will always feel how we want to feel. Take the list from the last prompt and figure out the feelings you get from imagining that perfect picture.

My perfect life feels like...

Day Fourteen   Gratitude   Date:

Today I am Most Grateful for:

1.

2.

3.

4.

5.

6.

7.

8.

9.

10.

I am so grateful that my twin flame and I...

What are your Deepest desires?

These are the things you've never revealed to anyone before. What do you want that you have never admitted to anyone? If you carry shame around these things, you will not achieve the union within that is required to achieve union without. You don't have to act on it or tell anyone about it. You just have to admit it to yourself. (It's okay. You can burn this page later if you need to. Just write it down!)

My deepest hidden desires are...

Day Fifteen   <u>Gratitude</u   Date:

Today I am Most Grateful for:

1.

2.

3.

4.

5.

6.

7.

8.

9.

10.

I am so grateful that my twin flame and I...

What are your greatest fears?

Fears we keep in the dark because we are afraid of them, actually control our lives. Same goes for shaming your deepest desires. You only need to admit these to yourself. You can burn this page later if you want.

My greatest fears are...

DAY SIXTEEN   GRATITUDE   DATE:

TODAY I AM MOST GRATEFUL FOR:

1.

2.

3.

4.

5.

6.

7.

8.

9.

10.

I AM SO GRATEFUL THAT MY TWIN FLAME AND I...

GUILTY PLEASURES

What things do you love that you are embarrassed about?

My guilty pleasures are...

Day Seventeen   <u>Gratitude</u   Date:

Today I am Most Grateful for:

1.

2.

3.

4.

5.

6.

7.

8.

9.

10.

I am so grateful that my twin flame and I...

Uprooting Shame

Let's get a little bit deeper now. To come into union with yourself and your twin, you have to learn to love the worst parts of yourself. What are you most ashamed of?

I am ashamed of...

Recognize that you did the best that you could with the light you had at the time. Try to find compassion and forgiveness for yourself.

I accept and forgive myself for...

Day Eighteen

<u>Gratitude</u>

Date:

Today I am Most Grateful for:

1.

2.

3.

4.

5.

6.

7.

8.

9.

10.

I am so grateful that my twin flame and I...

the Divine Masculine

Your feelings about the divine masculine within and without often mirror your relationships to the significant men in your life. Describe your relationship with your father.

My relationship with my father was/is...

My relationship with my own divine masculine mirrors that in these ways...

Day Nineteen GRATITUDE Date:

Today I am Most Grateful for:

1.

2.

3.

4.

5.

6.

7.

8.

9.

10.

I AM SO GRATEFUL THAT MY TWIN FLAME AND I...

the Divine Feminine

Your feelings about the divine Feminine within and without often mirror your relationships to the significant women in your life. Describe your relationship with your mother.

My relationship with my mother was/is...

My relationship with my own divine feminine mirrors that in these ways...

Day Twenty   GRATITUDE   Date:

Today I am Most Grateful for:

1.

2.

3.

4.

5.

6.

7.

8.

9.

10.

I am so grateful that my twin flame and I...

Big Money

To achieve harmonious union with your divine counterpart, you will need to examine your relationship to all things. The relationship to money can reveal hidden blocks to receiving abundance, which can also block you from receiving the abundant love of your twin flame union.

My relationship with money is...

Things I can do to improve my relationship with money are...

"My soul and your soul are forever tangled."

-N.R. Hart

Twin Flame Tip

Separation is an illusion created by the need to individuate in this reality. You are not, nor will you ever be separate in energetic reality.

Day Twenty-One   Gratitude   Date:

Today I am Most Grateful for:

1.

2.

3.

4.

5.

6.

7.

8.

9.

10.

I am so grateful that my twin flame and I...

Ghosts of Past Love

Think briefly about all your past significant relationships. List all the ones that still have a negative emotional charge.

I have the strongest emotional reactions to these three people

1.

2.

3.

The dominant emotions are

1.

2.

3.

Day Twenty-Two   <u>Gratitude</u>   Date:

Today I am Most Grateful for:

1.

2.

3.

4.

5.

6.

7.

8.

9.

10.

I am so grateful that my twin flame and I...

Cord Cutting Person #1

Grab a pencil with an eraser. Take a few deep breaths and center yourself. Intuitively tune into each of your chakras. Draw a line to where you feel there are energetic cords still attached to the other person.

CROWN

THIRD EYE

THROAT

HEART

SOLAR PLEXUS

SACRAL

ROOT

You

CROWN

THIRD EYE

THROAT

HEART

SOLAR PLEXUS

SACRAL

ROOT

Them

Call upon your guides and especially Archangel Michael. Tune in to each of your chakras one at a time. Ask that any cords or attachments you identified be lovingly removed, transmuted and sealed with light. Erase each line as you breathe and feel the cord of energy being cleansed and removed. If you feel you need it, you can remove the page and burn it.

Day Twenty-Three   Gratitude   Date:

Today I am Most Grateful for:

1.

2.

3.

4.

5.

6.

7.

8.

9.

10.

I am so grateful that my twin flame and I...

Cord Cutting Person #2

Grab a pencil with an eraser. Take a few deep breaths and center yourself. Intuitively tune into each of your chakras. Draw a line to where you feel there are energetic cords still attached to the other person.

CROWN	CROWN
THIRD EYE	THIRD EYE
THROAT	THROAT
HEART	HEART
SOLAR PLEXUS	SOLAR PLEXUS
SACRAL	SACRAL
ROOT	ROOT
You	**Them**

Call upon your guides and especially Archangel Michael. Tune in to each of your chakras one at a time. Ask that any cords or attachments you identified be lovingly removed, transmuted and sealed with light. Erase each line as you breathe and feel the cord of energy being cleansed and removed. If you feel you need it, you can remove the page and burn it.

Day Twenty-Four   GRATITUDE   Date:

Today I am Most Grateful for:

1.

2.

3.

4.

5.

6.

7.

8.

9.

10.

I am so grateful that my twin flame and I...

Cord Cutting Person #3

Grab a pencil with an eraser. Take a few deep breaths and center yourself. Intuitively tune into each of your chakras. Draw a line to where you feel there are energetic cords still attached to the other person.

CROWN

THIRD EYE

THROAT

HEART

SOLAR PLEXUS

SACRAL

ROOT

You

CROWN

THIRD EYE

THROAT

HEART

SOLAR PLEXUS

SACRAL

ROOT

Them

Call upon your guides and especially Archangel Michael. Tune in to each of your chakras one at a time. Ask that any cords or attachments you identified be lovingly removed, transmuted and sealed with light. Erase each line as you breathe and feel the cord of energy being cleansed and removed. If you feel you need it, you can remove the page and burn it.

Day Twenty-Five   <u>Gratitude</u   Date:

Today I am Most Grateful for:

1.

2.

3.

4.

5.

6.

7.

8.

9.

10.

I am so grateful that my twin flame and I...

Twin Flame Cord Cutting

Even though you can never cut the cord that binds you as souls, it is beneficial to remove any ego based attachments to assist the reunion process. Call Upon their higher self to assist you. Use the same method as before.

CROWN

THIRD EYE

THROAT

HEART

SOLAR PLEXUS

SACRAL

ROOT

YOU

CROWN

THIRD EYE

THROAT

HEART

SOLAR PLEXUS

SACRAL

ROOT

THEM

Day Twenty-six   <u>Gratitude</u>   Date:

Today I am Most Grateful for:

1.

2.

3.

4.

5.

6.

7.

8.

9.

10.

I am so grateful that my twin flame and I...

Cord Cutting Review

Write you experiences and thoughts about the cord cutting you have done over the past few days. Notice the shift in the emotional charge when you think about the people now, versus what it was like before.

Before the cord cutting I felt...

Now I feel...

Day Twenty-seven   Gratitude   Date:

Today I am Most Grateful for:

1.

2.

3.

4.

5.

6.

7.

8.

9.

10.

I am so grateful that my twin flame and I...

Letter from your inner child

Write from the perspective of your inner child. What messages do they have for you? What do they want or need? Writing with your non-dominant hand will help them express their voice.

Dear Grown up me,

Day Twenty-eight   <u>Gratitude</u   Date:

Today I am Most Grateful for:

1.

2.

3.

4.

5.

6.

7.

8.

9.

10.

I am so grateful that my twin flame and I...

Letter from your Twin's Inner Child

Write from the perspective of your Twin's inner child. What messages do they have for you? What do they want or need? Writing with your non-dominant hand will help them express their voice.

Dear beloved Twin Flame,

Day Twenty-Nine   Gratitude   Date:

Today I am Most Grateful for:

1.

2.

3.

4.

5.

6.

7.

8.

9.

10.

I am so grateful that my twin flame and I...

Anger

What are you still angry about? What upsets you most about being in separation from your beloved?

I am really angry that...

Day Thirty   Gratitude   Date:

Today I am Most Grateful for:

1.

2.

3.

4.

5.

6.

7.

8.

9.

10.

I am so grateful that my twin flame and I...

Sadness

What are you sad about? What have you not allowed yourself to grieve or mourn during this separation?

I am really sad that...

"The bond between twin flames is a sacred one. It's an alchemical marriage of the highest order"

-Unknown

Twin Flame Tip

On the soul level you are always in union. Staying connected to that reality will bring your physical reunion to you faster.

Day Thirty-One   Gratitude   Date:

Today I am Most Grateful for:

1.

2.

3.

4.

5.

6.

7.

8.

9.

10.

I am so grateful that my twin flame and I...

No regrets

Any regrets you have about your past are places where you are judging instead of loving yourself. Think about your life up until now. Are there things you would do differently and Why? What can you do, if anything, to change or improve in the future?

What I regret the most is...

I regret but can forgive myself for...

Day Thirty-Two   <u>Gratitude</u   Date:

Today I am Most Grateful for:

1.

2.

3.

4.

5.

6.

7.

8.

9.

10.

I am so grateful that my twin flame and I...

Past Script re-write

We can't change the past. Or can we? Write about a negative situation you wished had gone differently. But instead of writing it how it was, write it the way you wanted it to be.

Day Thirty-Three   <u>Gratitude</u>   Date:

Today I am Most Grateful for:

1.

2.

3.

4.

5.

6.

7.

8.

9.

10.

I am so grateful that my twin flame and I...

The Real You

Who are you when no one is looking? Compare and contrast who you are when you are around different kinds of people. How is it different than how you are when you're alone?

When I'm around strangers I am...

Around my friends I am...

With my lovers I am...

When I'm alone I am...

Day Thirty-Four   Gratitude   Date:

Today I am Most Grateful for:

1.

2.

3.

4.

5.

6.

7.

8.

9.

10.

I AM SO GRATEFUL THAT MY TWIN FLAME AND I...

Life Purpose

What would you be doing right now if money didn't matter? What about if acceptance or approval didn't matter? What if people's opinions didn't matter?

If none of that mattered I would be...

If none of that mattered I would do...

Day Thirty-Five   GRATITUDE   DATE:

TODAY I AM MOST GRATEFUL FOR:

1.

2.

3.

4.

5.

6.

7.

8.

9.

10.

I AM SO GRATEFUL THAT MY TWIN FLAME AND I...

What's the roadblock?

What's really in the way of you being what you really want to be? What's really in the way of you doing what you want to do?

I can't be who I want to be because...

I can't do what I want to do because...

Is that true? Is it absolutely true? How do you know it's absolutely true?

Day Thirty-Six   GRATITUDE   Date:

Today I am Most Grateful for:

1.

2.

3.

4.

5.

6.

7.

8.

9.

10.

I am so grateful that my twin flame and I...

Conflicting Desires

No matter how much you say you want something, if a part of you wants something else more, or thinks something else you want is in opposition, you won't get the thing you say you want. What do you want that you think you can't have if you were in harmonious union right now? What do you not want that you think will come along with the union you seek?

I want harmonious union, but I also really want..

I want harmonious union, but I really don't want...

Is there a way that you can have all the things that you want, and avoid what you don't want?

If not, can you accept what is as it is?

Day Thirty-Seven   Gratitude   Date:

Today I am Most Grateful for:

1.

2.

3.

4.

5.

6.

7.

8.

9.

10.

I am so grateful that my twin flame and I...

The Part of Separation

It's time to address the part of you that has chosen separation. Nothing happens to you, it only happens for you. Write from the perspective of the part(s) that want this separation. Understand its fears and hesitations. What does this part of you want or need in order to make a new choice towards union?

The part of me that wants separation needs...

How I will help this part of me is...

Day Thirty-Eight   Gratitude   Date:

Today I am Most Grateful for:

1.

2.

3.

4.

5.

6.

7.

8.

9.

10.

I am so grateful that my twin flame and I...

Masks Off

Write from the perspective of the part(s) of you that is afraid to let you express yourself authentically. What is it afraid of? What will happen if you are your most authentic self? What does it need to feel safe to allow you to do so?

The part of me that is scared to let me be my authentic self wants...

What I will do to make them feel safe is...

Day Thirty-Nine   Gratitude   Date:

Today I am Most Grateful for:

1.

2.

3.

4.

5.

6.

7.

8.

9.

10.

I am so grateful that my twin flame and I...

Open to Receive

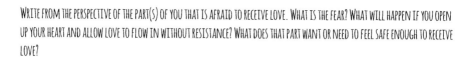

Write from the perspective of the part(s) of you that is afraid to receive love. What is the fear? What will happen if you open up your heart and allow love to flow in without resistance? What does that part want or need to feel safe enough to receive love?

The part of me afraid of love needs...

What I will provide for this part is...

Day Forty   Gratitude   Date:

Today I am Most Grateful for:

1.

2.

3.

4.

5.

6.

7.

8.

9.

10.

I am so grateful that my twin flame and I...

Leave Me Alone

Write from the perspective of the part of you that wants to be alone. What is it afraid will happen if you are in partnership with your divine beloved? What does it want or need to feel safe enough to share itself with your twin soul?

The part of me that wants to be alone is afraid of...

What I will give to this part is...

"I AM CONSTANTLY SURPRISED BY THE LONGING FOR YOU THAT NEVER QUIETS."

-TYLER KNOTT GREGSON

Twin Flame Tip

Your twin flame is you. When you miss them, you are missing yourself. Anything you do that drops you deeper into your own essence, brings you even closer to union.

Day Forty-One   GRATITUDE   DATE:

TODAY I AM MOST GRATEFUL FOR:

1.

2.

3.

4.

5.

6.

7.

8.

9.

10.

I AM SO GRATEFUL THAT MY TWIN FLAME AND I...

Too Hot to Handle

Write from the perspective of the part that is afraid of the sexual intensity of the connection. Ask it what it needs to be open to receiving the magnitude of the pleasure available through divine union. What perspective does it need to be excited instead of nervous or overwhelmed?

The part of me afraid of the sexual connection wants...

What I will do to help this part is...

Day Forty-Two   <u>Gratitude</u   Date:

Today I am Most Grateful for:

1.

2.

3.

4.

5.

6.

7.

8.

9.

10.

I am so grateful that my twin flame and I...

Lifetimes Apart

Write down all the lifetimes you chose separation and why. Embracing that it is your free will choice, gives you the power to make the choice toward union instead. If separation is not of your own doing then you can't undo it. Take responsibility and the power to change it is yours once more.

In some lifetimes I chose separation because...

In other lifetimes I chose separation because...

In yet other lifetimes I chose separation because...

I am choosing separation in this life because...

Day Forty-Three   GRATITUDE   Date:

Today I am Most Grateful for:

1.

2.

3.

4.

5.

6.

7.

8.

9.

10.

I am so grateful that my twin flame and I...

Releasing Emotions

Whatever thoughts, beliefs, and/or feelings that are still lingering about your time in separation, purge them now.

I still feel...

How I want to feel is...

Day Forty-Four   <u>Gratitude</u   Date:

Today I am Most Grateful for:

1.

2.

3.

4.

5.

6.

7.

8.

9.

10.

I am so grateful that my twin flame and I...

Cutting Ties With Past Lives

Ask your higher self, "What do I need to know or be aware of in order to release all past lives of separation?"

The lessons I need to integrate are...

Day Forty-Five   <u>Gratitude</u>   Date:

Today I am Most Grateful for:

1.

2.

3.

4.

5.

6.

7.

8.

9.

10.

I am so grateful that my twin flame and I...

I don't want to

Write from the perspective of any part that is still resistant to union, or who doesn't want to heal the separation. What is it afraid of? What does it want or need to feel safe to complete this process?

The part of me still in resistance needs...

What I will give to this part is...

Day Forty-Six   <u>Gratitude</u>   Date:

Today I am Most Grateful for:

1.

2.

3.

4.

5.

6.

7.

8.

9.

10.

I am so grateful that my twin flame and I...

I am Lovable

List all the things you like and/or love about yourself.

I like that I am...

I love that I am...

Day Forty-Seven   Gratitude   Date:

Today I am Most Grateful for:

1.

2.

3.

4.

5.

6.

7.

8.

9.

10.

I am so grateful that my twin flame and I...

Room for Improvement

Write the things you dislike most about yourself.

I really don't like that I...

I hate that I...

Actions I can take to improve these things are...

Day Forty-Eight   <u>Gratitude</u>   Date:

Today I am Most Grateful for:

1.

2.

3.

4.

5.

6.

7.

8.

9.

10.

I am so grateful that my twin flame and I...

Know Your Why

Why do you want union with your Twin? What do you expect to feel? How will your life change as a result?

I want harmonious union with my twin flame because I want to feel...

Things I can do to feel these ways now are...

Day Forty-Nine   <u>Gratitude</u>   Date:

Today I am Most Grateful for:

1.

2.

3.

4.

5.

6.

7.

8.

9.

10.

I am so grateful that my twin flame and I...

What if you Never

What if you never achieve union? Imagine that for a moment. Don't dwell on it, but it is important to face this fear. How would you feel? Could you continue on with your life? Could you find ways to be happy without them? Would you be okay? Would you survive?

If my twin flame and I never reach harmonious union then I would....

Is that true?

DAY FIFTY   GRATITUDE   DATE:

TODAY I AM MOST GRATEFUL FOR:

1.

2.

3.

4.

5.

6.

7.

8.

9.

10.

I AM SO GRATEFUL THAT MY TWIN FLAME AND I...

Claim Your Union

Now that you can see you will survive if you never achieve union, you can fully and completely claim it. Now it is a conscious free will choice and no longer a desperate need to feel better or avoid pain. Write any version of declaring a claim to union. Some examples are, "I (state your name) claim my harmonious twin flame union now!""Harmonious Union is already mine and I officially claim it!" Seal it with your signature and a kiss.

"When I met you, I found me."

-Unknown

Twin Flame Tip

Being with your twin feels like nothing else you've ever felt. It feels like blissful and peaceful solitude. It's like being by yourself. Because they are literally just more of you inside another body.

Day Fifty-One   <u>Gratitude</u>   Date:

Today I am Most Grateful for:

1.

2.

3.

4.

5.

6.

7.

8.

9.

10.

I AM SO GRATEFUL THAT MY TWIN FLAME AND I...

Divine Love

Twin flame union is a divine love. It is also Divine union with source. Describe your relationship with Source, God, Higher Power...etc. Notice anything that needs to be addressed.

My relationship with God/Source/Universe...etc. is...

This mirrors my twin flame journey in these ways...

Day Fifty-Two   Gratitude   Date:

Today I am Most Grateful for:

1.

2.

3.

4.

5.

6.

7.

8.

9.

10.

I AM SO GRATEFUL THAT MY TWIN FLAME AND I...

Mr. & Mrs. Doubtfire

Allow the part of you that still has doubts, hesitations, or concerns to speak now. Is there a part of you that doesn't believe union is possible? Why Not? What does it want or need to have complete faith and sound belief?

This part of me has doubts or disbelief because...

What I will do to help this part is...

Day Fifty-Three   <u>Gratitude</u   Date:

Today I am Most Grateful for:

1.

2.

3.

4.

5.

6.

7.

8.

9.

10.

I am so grateful that my twin flame and I...

Sacred Sex

Quiet your mind. Take some deep cleansing breaths. Imagine a highly sensual or sexual encounter with your twin. Feel all the way into it. Use all of your senses. Notice what emotions or feelings rise to the surface. Is it easy to imagine? Is it difficult? Do you feel any sexual guilt or shame? Is the pleasure overwhelming? How do you feel before, during and after?

My experience connecting with my twin sexually is...

Day Fifty-Four   <u>Gratitude</u>   Date:

Today I am Most Grateful for:

1.

2.

3.

4.

5.

6.

7.

8.

9.

10.

I AM SO GRATEFUL THAT MY TWIN FLAME AND I...

Body Language

How is your relationship with your body? Take some deep breaths and close your eyes. Tune into your physical body. How does it feel? Notice any areas of tension or pain. Are there things you love about it? What would you change?

My relationship with my body is...

Things I can do to love my body more are...

Day Fifty-Five   <u>Gratitude</u>   Date:

Today I am Most Grateful for:

1.

2.

3.

4.

5.

6.

7.

8.

9.

10.

I am so grateful that my twin flame and I...

Body Talk

Write from the perspective of your body. Allow it to give you messages or communicate to you what it wants and needs. Is it feeling nourished or neglected? Does it have any special requests for you? What does it want more of? What does it want less of? How does it feel about you and why?

Dear Self,

Day Fifty-Six   GRATITUDE   DATE:

Today I am Most Grateful for:

1.

2.

3.

4.

5.

6.

7.

8.

9.

10.

I AM SO GRATEFUL THAT MY TWIN FLAME AND I...

Holding On

What are you still holding onto? Where do you feel the most tension in your body? Breathe into that place. What messages does it have for you?

I am still holding on to...

What I need to let go of is...

How I will do this is...

Day Fifty-Seven   <u>Gratitude</u>   Date:

Today I am Most Grateful for:

1.

2.

3.

4.

5.

6.

7.

8.

9.

10.

I am so grateful that my twin flame and I...

LET'S BE HONEST

Sometimes we filter ourselves, even when no one is watching. Free write after the following prompt without judgement. Write literally everything that comes to your mind. You can burn this page later if you want.

If I were to be completely honest...

Day Fifty-Eight   <u>Gratitude</u>   Date:

Today I am Most Grateful for:

1.

2.

3.

4.

5.

6.

7.

8.

9.

10.

I am so grateful that my twin flame and I...

Confessions

This is along the same lines as the last one, but from a different angle. It's time for some confessions. Write with zero filter or judgments. You can burn this later if you need to.

I don't really want to admit it but...

Day Fifty-Nine

<u>Gratitude</u>

Date:

Today I am Most Grateful for:

1.

2.

3.

4.

5.

6.

7.

8.

9.

10.

I am so grateful that my twin flame and I...

Positive Changes

What is something you are still not happy with or about? What can you do to move towards positive changes in the area?

Something I'm still not happy with is...

Some action steps I intend on taking are...

Day Sixty

<u>Gratitude</u>

Date:

Today I am Most Grateful for:

1.

2.

3.

4.

5.

6.

7.

8.

9.

10.

I am so grateful that my twin flame and I...

The Recap

You made it! Congratulations. Honor and thank yourself for showing up everyday and doing this work. Reflect back on your journey these last sixty days. How did you feel about your union when you began? How do you feel about it now? What was the state of your reality before you started? How is it now? What still hasn't changed? What can you do to make improvements in that area?

When I began this journey I...

Now I...

"When love runs soul deep, a kiss is no longer just a kiss. It is the place where heaven and earth meet."

-Daniel Nielsen

Twin Flame Tip

True twin Flames share Core Values and Decisions. If you are doing healing work, they will shift as well. If you avoid doing deep work, so will they. If you run from yourself, they will run from you. If you choose union with yourself, they will choose union with you too.

"You don't find love, it finds you. It's got a little bit to do with destiny, fate, and what's written in the stars."

-Anaïs Nin

Twin Flame tip

You don't have to create your union. It already exists. you only need to remove what is in the way of you seeing it, feeling it, and being it.

"Lovers don't finally meet somewhere. They're in each other all along."

-Rumi

Twin Flame Union Guided Journal

60 Days of Gratitude and Self Reflection

Thank you again for letting me be your guide on this journey! If you found this enjoyable or helpful in any way, please share with a friend, and check out gonegoddess.com for more books, teachings, and courses.

See you Again Soon!

xoxo Gone Goddess

Printed in Great Britain
by Amazon